Naïve & Abroad:
Israel & Palestine

Naïve & Abroad: Israel & Palestine

✦

Obvious Questions No One Asks

Marcus Henderson Wilder

iUniverse, Inc.
New York   Bloomington

Naïve & Abroad: Israel & Palestine
Obvious Questions No One Asks

iUniverse books may be ordered through booksellers or by contacting:

iUniverse
1663 Liberty Drive
Bloomington, IN 47403
www.iuniverse.com
1-800-Authors (1-800-288-4677)

ISBN: 978-1-4401-3512-5 (sc)
ISBN: 978-1-4401-3513-2 (ebook)

Printed in the United States of America

iUniverse rev. date: 3/30/2009

**Naïve &
Abroad**

Contents

**Naïve &
Abroad**

Naked Data

The 1844 census of Jerusalem found 7120 Jews…5760 Muslims…3390 Christians.

In 1869, Mark Twain wrote of the emptiness of the land. Mark Twain wrote of Arab sloth and filth and flies.

In the 1880s, Americans forced Indians from their land to resettle Indian land with whites. Many Indians had to be killed.

In the 1880s, Australians forced Aborigines from their land to resettle Aborigine land with whites. Many Aborigines had to be killed.

In the 1880s, white New Zealanders forced Maoris from their land to resettle Maori land with whites. Many Maoris had to be killed.

In the 1880s, European Jews *bought* idle land in what is now Israel, *joining Mizrahi Jews continuously there since Abraham.*

Beginning in 1882, forty Jewish families settled at Rishon L'Tzion. *Four hundred* Arab families settled around them. Some of the Arab families were Bedouin. Some came from Egypt.

A British official reported Arabs sought employment, clean drinking water, better health care, and lower infant mortality. The official reported this pattern repeated everywhere Jews settled.

In the 1890s, Belgians cut off the hands of Africans who did not gather enough rubber.

In the 1890s, Arabs flocked to Jewish areas of Palestine for jobs created by Jewish investment and enterprise.

After WWI, Britain tried to set up a Palestinian governing body of twelve…eight Arabs…two Christians…two Jews. Arabs said two Jews were too many. A cynic might say Arabs knew then two Jews outnumbered eight Arabs.

In 1917, the British Balfour Agreement promised a national home for Jews in Palestine. The British did not mean it.

Arabs turned down two-state solutions in 1917, 1937, 1948, and 2000.

After a Nazi supported Arab revolt in 1936-1939, British-backed Arab religious leader Husseini fled to Germany. Husseini is revered throughout Islam today.

In 1939, A British White Paper severely restricted Jewish immigration into Palestine.

After WWII, European Jews sought refuge in what is now Israel. The Arabist British did all they could to keep Jews out of Palestine. Under United Nations mandate, Jews established the State of Israel despite Arab objections and British perfidy.

In the United Nations document authorizing the formation of the state of Israel, an Arab/British/African clause weighted population numbers in favor of Arabs. In 1948, the Arab population was still largely transient. This clause identified any Arab who had been in Palestine for two years a permanent resident.

Do we give casual Mexican labor citizenship after two years in the United States?

In 1948, Arab countries attacked the infant Jewish nation. Jewish citizen soldiers decisively defeated combined professional armies of five Arab nations.

In 1948, a disputed number of Arab residents of Israel fled and/or were expelled. There is evidence Arabs residents were encouraged *by Arab invaders* to flee to give Arab invaders a freer hand.

Only Jordan offered refugees citizenship. In all other Muslim countries, Palestinian refugees remain in camps *sixty years later*...anti-Israeli propaganda pawns.

In the months following the 1948 war, 850,000 Sephardic/Mizrahi Jews fled or were expelled to Israel from Arab countries. We do not know how many Jews fled to other nations. We do not know how many Jews were killed. Arab nations claim no knowledge of this flight/expulsion.

Sephardic Jews had been in the Middle East since 1492, Mizrahi Jews since Abraham.

If Palestinians wanted their own country, Palestinians would call a constitutional convention...write a governing document...declare a nation. There is precedent.

If Palestinians wanted their own country, Palestinians would call a constitutional convention...write a governing document...declare a nation. There is precedent.

Since the 1967 War, Palestinian Muslims have been called Palestinians. Palestinians are Arab-speakers...not Arabs. Palestinians are probably Turkish Hittites who reached Palestine via Crete and Cyprus. Palestinian origins are uncertain.

Palestinians are the Philistines of the Bible...the Sea People. What is now Gaza was Philistia. Gaza is theirs...unless Gaza belongs to Canaanite peoples Philistines displaced...peoples who had been there since time before memory.

Romans called the province Palestine to insult rebellious Jews. Ottomans kept the name.

If Palestinians had lived in peace beside Jews in democratic Israel, Palestinians would own Israel. With the differential in birth rates, Palestinians could have taken democratic Israel with the vote.

The story of modern Israel & Palestine is not what we are told.

Palestinian leader Musa Alami said in 1948, "The people are in great need of a myth to fill their consciousness and imagination."

The King of Jordan denied displacement of Arabs by Jewish settlements. The king said, "The Arabs are as prodigal in selling their land as they are in…weeping [about it].

The popular history of Palestine is myth.

Naïve & Abroad

Who are Palestinians?

Palestinians may be Homer's Greek Heroes.

Palestinians may be Turkish Hittites. Hittite origins are uncertain.

Before about 1200 BC the record is murky. A good story can be built around every theory. I find no DNA studies.

On firmer historical ground, the Philistines - the Sea People - invaded what is now Palestine.

Philistines raided are far as Egypt before Egyptian war chariots stopped that.

The Sea People worked iron. Their closely guarded knowledge of iron gave them superior weapons. Philistines used iron weapons against Jews with great effect until defeated by King David.

One story has Philistines coming to Palestine from Crete, which would make them Cretans...*terrible pun.*

A second story has Philistines coming from Cyprus.

Arguments are made iron was worked on Cyprus and not on Crete. A counter-argument says Crete exported copper so metalworking must have been known there.

Recent excavations support both theories. Pottery is not a reliable indicator of origin. Similar pottery was traded and used all around the eastern Mediterranean.

Whatever their origins, Philistines invaded what is now Gaza about 1200 BC. They clashed immediately with Jews. Philistines got the best of it until David defeated them.

Goliath was Philistine.

David incorporated Philistine units into his army.

The Bible account of the history of the period is accurate. There is no Philistine record.

Homer's account overlaps Bible history.

After their defeat by David, Philistines faded into the Palestinian background until European Jewish settlement began in the 1880s. Philistines reappear as migrant workers drawn to jobs in 1880s Jewish agriculture and industry.

What is now Gaza was Philistia. It might be claimed Gaza belongs to Palestinians…unless Gaza belongs to Canaanites Philistines displaced.

Philistines adopted Canaanite culture and customs. Canaanites practiced child sacrifice.

We take our word sodomy from the Canaanite city of Sodom.

Naïve & Abroad

Why Do Palestinians Not Have a Country?

The short answer is Palestinians do not want their own country. Palestinians want Israel…Israel without Jews.

Palestinians could have their own sovereign nation within weeks by calling a constitutional convention…writing a governing document…declaring a nation. There is precedent.

Palestinians could have their own sovereign nation within weeks by calling a constitutional convention…writing a governing document…declaring a nation. There is precedent.

Every nation in the world would recognize Palestinian sovereignty. Aid and investment would flood in from everywhere, *including from Israel.* Palestinian prosperity would be assured.

Half the nations of the world would guarantee the safety of the new nation.

Palestinians rejected two state solutions in 1917, 1937, 1948, and 2000.

Palestinians rejected a country of their own in 1917, 1937, 1948, and

2000.

Cynics say the 1917 British Balfour proposal of a homeland for Jews in Palestine was a ploy to attract support of world Jewry in WWI.

Balfour angered Arabs.

In 1937 the British Peel Commission recommended division of the land into two countries. A map was presented with Peel proposals.

Jews quickly agreed in principal, with details to be negotiated.

Palestinians would not grant citizenship to nor guarantee safety of Jews who would - because of where they lived - become residents of the proposed Palestinian nation.

A key Palestinian demand was that Jews not be allowed to buy land anywhere.

Palestinians refused a Palestinian state.

British need for oil outweighed every moral consideration. To appease Arabs, the British withdrew the Peel proposals. British Arabists - and therefore Arabs - have controlled British Middle East policy since.

Churchill stood up for Jews. Churchill was soon gone.

When Israel was formed in 1948, creation of a Palestinian state was again proposed.

Palestinians and their Arab allies preferred elimination of Israel with war.

In 2000, Israeli leader Ehud Barak offered Palestinians the moon at Camp David.

Yasser Arafat turned down a package *that included more than he demanded.* Cynics said Arafat would be killed by his own supporters if he agreed to *anything* Barak proposed.

Nothing but destruction of Israel and death or expulsion of Jews will satisfy Palestinians.

**Naïve &
Abroad**

Why Do Arab Countries Not Accept Palestinian Refugees?

There are two reasons Palestinians are kept in refugee camps sixty years after fleeing Israel.

Impoverished, suffering Palestinian refugees are propaganda tools.

A cynic might say anti-Israeli U.S. news organizations would suffer without news stories of suffering Palestinians.

Other Muslims do not trust Palestinians. Diplomat and Brigadier General Ramatullah Safi told me every educated Muslim *loathes* Palestinians. No one dares say it.

Only tiny Jordan made Palestinian refugees citizens.

Palestinians attempted to overthrow the government. The loyalty of the Bedouin army prevented Palestinian takeover of Jordan.

Palestinian refugee camps are further evidence Arab countries expect Israel to go away one day.

**Naïve &
Abroad**

Who are Sunni and Shi'a?

Sunni and Shi'a are rival Muslim groups. Sunni are considered mainstream Islam by everyone but Shi'a. Shi'a are considered a breakaway sect by everyone but Shi'a.

Ali married Mohammed's daughter, Fatima. Ali and his followers believed Ali was the rightful caliph - ruler - of all Islam after Mohammed's death. Aisha, Mohammed's favorite wife, opposed Ali.

There were wars, murders, plots, schemes, bribery, and betrayals... more than enough to fill this small book. Ali forces defeated Aisha forces in a war. Ali allowed Aisha to go home to Medina. Aisha is not heard from again.

Ali became caliph after his predecessor and rival was stabbed to death at prayer.

Ali then engaged in a war with another rival. The rival's soldiers stuck pages of the Koran on the heads of their spears. Ali's men would not fight the Koran. Ali had to cut a political deal with the rival.

The political deal enraged Ali's supporters supporters. One of his supporters stabbed Ali dead.

After this the story is complicated as only Arab intrigue can be complicated.

Out of these intrigues came the belief that Ali's descendents were cheated of the caliphate. *Ali's descendents were bought off with cash and pensions.*

Shi'a believe it is the fault of the Sunni Ali's descendents are not caliphs. Hatred of Sunnis runs deep.

Resentment is an important part of being Shi'a, followers of Ali.

Naïve & Abroad

Who are Hamas and Hezbollah?

By any reasonable measure, Hamas and Hezbollah are terrorist organizations.

Muslims do not see it that way.

Each organization wears three hats. Each is a charity. Each is a political party. Each is a terrorist organization sworn to destroy Israel.

Hamas is Sunni. Hamas operates primarily in Gaza. Hamas newly has Iranian support.

Hezbollah is Shi'a. Hezbollah operates primarily in Lebanon. Hezbollah is de facto an extension of Iran. Hezbollah is now part of the Lebanese political power structure.

Both organizations get military training and money from Iran.

Part of the power of these organizations with the Arab street is their *claimed* incorruptibility.

One of the major advantages of these organizations is the Islamic requirement that Muslims give 2% to charity. It is not clear to me 2% of what. Whatever the measure, enormous sums are paid to Hamas and Hezbollah charities.

Both organizations operate effective, highly-visible, *apparently* incorruptible charities. The people of Gaza and Lebanon are seen to benefit from schools, hospitals, food aid, and much else the poor need.

Unfortunately, more charity money goes to buy guns and rockets than to buy schoolbooks or medicines or food. The people do not care. The destruction of Israel is dear to Palestinian and Lebanese Muslim hearts.

The destruction of Israel is dear to Palestinian and Lebanese Muslim hearts.

Who is Fatah?

Fatah is the reverse acronym of Palestinian National Liberation Movement, a member party of the Palestinian Liberation Organization, the PLO, famously led by Yasser Arafat.

Fatah is - astonishingly to me - not listed as a terrorist organization.

Fatah is nationalistic and semi-Leftist.

Nazi-ism and *Fascism* are nationalistic and semi-Leftist…and hate Jews.

Fatah is *stupendously* corrupt. Hundreds of millions of aid dollars - perhaps billions of aid dollars - disappear into Fatah leadership Swiss bank accounts.

Fatah has sub-groups.

Fatah employs militias of varying incompetence.

Fatah supports terrorist groups with charity and aid money.

Fatah corruption led to the rise of Hamas.

We support Fatah politically and financially. Politics make strange bedfellows. Fatah will deal so we deal with Fatah.

We take what we can get.

Naïve & Abroad

Who Are the Jews?

Jews [and Arabs] are children of Abraham.

There are three major Jewish ethnic groups…three minor ethnic groups…and other groups almost too small to count.

Nearly all Jews are interconnected by DNA links.

The Jews most of us know are European Ashkenazi Jews. The Ashkenazim are Turkic Russians. The Cohen DNA thread runs unbroken from Jerusalem through Europe to New York and Sydney and Buenos Aires. Some DNA tests suggest distant connection to Kurds.

This is not the place for the Khazar Controversy. I accept H.G. Wells's version of the story.

The second largest group is Sephardic Jews, Jews of Spain. The DNA thread is again unbroken.

I have a chapter on the persecution and expulsion of Sephardic Jews from Spain in *Naïve & Abroad: Spain, Limping 600 Miles through History*. I have a chapter in *Naïve & Abroad: Mexico, Painted Mask* on why many upper class Mexicans are descendents of Sephardic Jews.

The smallest of the major groups is Mizrahi Jews. These are Jews continuously in the Middle East since Abraham.

There are many fewer Yemeni Jews. The black Jewish tribe in South Africa has DNA links to Yemeni Jews.

Ethiopian Jews are black, but not related to the South African tribe. Nearly all Ethiopian Jews were airlifted to Israel to escape persecution.

There are still fewer Indian Jews, refugees from the expulsion of Jews from Portugal. These are related to Sephardic Jews.

There is a tiny group of Jews - probably Sephardic - in China.

There are Iraqi Jews, Berber Jews, Kurdish Jews, Mountain Jews, and Georgian Jews. Most practice Sephardic rites. This is traced to Sephardic flight from Iberia. Some Mizrahim adopted Sephardic rituals.

Some of the Moorish tribes who invaded Spain were converts to Judaism.

The question of who *is* a Jew - as opposed to who *are* the Jews - is not important here. The question of who *is* a Jew is a family fight. Ask a Jewish friend to explain it.

Since Palestinians are not Arabs, Palestinians are not children of Abraham.

Naïve & Abroad

Why Does Israel Build a Wall?

Israel builds a wall to keep out suicide/homicide bombers. The wall has effectively stopped suicide/homicide bombing attacks.

Building the wall uses funds that could be used to build roads or schools or hospitals. Israel does not build the wall for amusement. If there were no suicide/homicide bombers there would be no wall.

Much is made of the damage done to Palestinian populations by the loss of trade with Israel. Israel loses trade as well.

Palestinians lose access to Israeli jobs. Israel loses Palestinian labor. Beneficial commerce is lost.

There are no winners in suicide/homicide bombings.

Much of the cement used in wall panels is bought from Palestinian cement plants.

**Naïve &
Abroad**

Why Does Israel Attack Gaza?

Israel attacks Gaza too stop the rockets. Were no rockets fired into Israel, Israel would not invade Gaza.

Military operations are expensive in lives and treasure. Because the world press sides with the rocketeers, Israeli invasions of Gaza are public relations disasters.

To stop Israeli invasions of Gaza, stop the rockets.

To stop Israeli attacks on Hamas leaders, stop the rockets.

This is not rocket science.

Much is made of disproportionate Israeli response to Palestinian rockets.

What is proportionate response…one rocket for one rocket?

**Naïve &
Abroad**

Why Does Israel Not Return Land Captured in the Six Days War?

Israel adjusted her borders to a line easier to defend.

This is a defense issue, not a land grab issue. Arab armies fled. Israel could have kept as much captured territory as she wanted.

We did not return *any* of the land we took from Mexico in the War of 1848? Taking northern Mexico was an unashamed land grab for which we are not embarrassed.

How many San Franciscans would give California back to Mexico?

Naïve & Abroad

Why Does Israel Not Return the Golan Heights to Syria?

Israel returned the Golan Heights once.

Syria moved artillery onto the heights and shelled Israel...again

What Happened in 1967?

Modern history of the Middle East began in 1967.

Egypt expelled UN peacekeepers from the Egyptian/Israeli border.

Egypt closed the Suez Canal to Israeli shipping.

Egypt massed 1,000 tanks and 100,000 soldiers in attack formation at the border. Israel preemptively attacked and destroyed the Egyptian air force. Egypt attacked across the Suez Canal. Jordan attacked Jerusalem. Syria, Iraq, and Saudi Arabia attacked from the rear.

Anti-Israelis - especially Leftists - use Israel's preemptive strike as further proof of Israeli aggression. Israelis attacked Arabs who were not doing anything to Israelis.

The war lasted six days. Many of us remember news photographs of Gen. Moshe Dyan wearing an eye patch. News films showed Egyptian rifles and tanks and boots abandoned in the sand as Egyptian soldiers fled barefoot across the Sinai desert toward the Suez Canal and Egypt.

At the beginning of the war, Israeli territory was tactically un-defendable. At one point, Israel was nine miles wide. An artillery shell could be fired from outside Israel on one side and hit a target *beyond Israel* on the other side.

Israel adjusted her borders. Israel will not give up this land. We will not give up Arizona or California to Mexico.

In 1967, Israel captured Gaza, the West Bank, the Golan Heights, East Jerusalem, and the Sinai Peninsula. Israel kept *only* land critical to national defense.

Israeli farmers tend vineyards and graze sheep around abandoned Syrian artillery positions in the Golan Heights.

Naïve & Abroad

Why Does Israel Build Settlements?

Forward settlements are classic defense strategy.

Catherine the Great established forward settlements along Russia's southern and western borders in a great arc from the Baltic States to Georgia. Best known are Volga Germans.

Romans positioned citizen infantry in forward settlements.

Americans colonies built forward settlements between settled areas and Indian Territory. Ft. Ticonderoga was a forward settlement.

Like so much recent history, Israeli settlements began after the 1967 war.

The first four settlements were built along a mountain ridge. Subsequent settlements were built along the border with Jordan and along the 1967 line of defense.

Israeli settlements occupy two percent of the West Bank. Critics say settlements *control* forty percent of West Bank territory. Exactly... settlements are the first line of Israeli defense.

No Israeli concessions stop the rockets. Removal of Israeli Gaza settlements encouraged terrorist belief they will win.

Illegal settlements by Israeli religious fanatics are another matter. Israel should be condemned for not moving more forcefully against illegal settlements.

Israeli political instability makes moving against illegal settlements difficult.

**Naïve &
Abroad**

Why does the United States support Israel?

If you have to ask, you will never get it.

Israel is Western civilization's forward outpost where religion teaches Infidels must be converted or killed.

You are the Infidel the Faithful must convert or kill.

Naïve & Abroad

Why Does Britain Side With Arabs?

Oil...and a tradition of anti-Semitism in the British governing classes....

Members of the British Royal Family supported Hitler.

Before marrying Edward, Prince of Wales, Wallis Warfield Simpson spied for the Nazis in Shanghai.

When Edward, Duke of Windsor, was Governor of the Bahamas, Nazi submarines re-provisioned in the Bahamas.

**Naïve &
Abroad**

What is Zionism?

Zionism is the belief Jews should have a homeland in Palestine.

Most civilized individuals agree.

The belief that Jews should have a homeland in Palestine is not new. Jews have long prayed, "…next year in Jerusalem…."

In the late 19th century, an Austro-Hungarian journalist formalized the belief and gave it a name. Theodor Herzl became father of Zionism.

Zionists encouraged Jewish migration to Palestine. Zionists were important in the formation of modern Israel in 1948.

Zionism is largely secular. Most early Zionists were Socialists. Socialism was the *idée du jure* for late 19th century intellectuals.

Jews may have a gene for Socialism.

Zionism's aims are benign.

Naïve & Abroad

What is Mossad?

Mossad is the Israeli CIA. The parallel is not exact.

Mossad is the best intelligence gathering organization in the world. Mossad excels at *humint,* intelligence gathered by spies. There is probably no organization in the world important to Israeli security not penetrated by Mossad.

Salon.com speculates Bill Clinton pardoned Marc Rich because Rich is/ was an important Mossad asset doing dangerous work and performing valuable services - valuable to both Israel and the United States - in countries where he does business.

Mossad enjoyed - and continues to enjoy - spectacular successes and - infrequently - humiliating failures.

Mossad successes include the kidnapping of Adoph Eichmann in Argentina. Eichman was a Nazi bureaucrat who coordinated shipping of Jews to concentration camps. Eichmann was taken to Israel for public trial.

Nearly all Mossad activities are deniable and denied. Eichman could have been killed quietly. Israel wanted public trial.

A Mossad team called Wrath of God hunted down and - one by one -

killed the assassins of the Israeli Olympic athletes at Munich.

One spectacular failure was the capture of two Mossad agents trying to squirt poison into the ear of a PLO terrorist leader in Amman, Jordan. I did not make that up.

No other organization is as hated by the enemies of Western civilization.

Tzipi Livni, prominent political leader, is a former Mossad operative.

Naïve & Abroad

What are the Protocols of the Elders of Zion?

Nothing should be this complicated.

The *Protocols of the Elders of Zion* claim to expose a Jewish plot for world domination.

A Scottish mathematician hated Freemasons.

In 1797, a French Jesuit priest named Abbe Barruel - influenced by the Scot - published a tract accusing Freemasons of anti-Royalist sympathies in France.

Since most Royalists were Freemasons, Barruel was forced to change his story. In the new version, Jews replaced Freemasons as the anti-Royalist evil.

In 1864, a French satirist, Maurice Joly, published a satirical political pamphlet - *Dialogues* -based on Barruel's revised version. Napoleon III, Joly wrote, was too easy on Jews. Joly went to jail for anti-government propaganda.

A German novelist, Hermann Goedsche, writing as Sir John Retcliffe, used Joly's *Dialogues* as the basis for claims of a Jewish world conspiracy in his *Biarritz* novels.

The *Biarritz* novels were the basis for the *Protocols of the Elders of Zion* written by a Russian secret police agent in Paris between 1895 and 1899. Parts of this work were privately published in 1897.

The first public printing of the complete *Protocols* was in Russia in 1905 by Sergei Nilus, a secret police agent. There were revised versions in 1906 and later.

The Tsar denounced the *Protocols* as false. The Tsar kept a beautifully bound copy of the 1906 version in his library.

Until the fall of the Tsar, the *Protocols* were published only in Russia. After the fall of the Tsar, both White Russians and Communists used the *Protocols* to foment more anti-Jewish pogroms.

Another Russian, Boris Brasol, brought the *Protocols* to Paris. The *Protocols* were translated into all major languages.

A Michigan newspaper founded by Henry Ford published the *Protocols* in 1920.

The *Protocols* were the foundation of Hitler's anti-Jewish propaganda.

The Times of London exposed the fraud in a four-part series in 1935.

The Protocols *live on wherever Jews are hated.*

**Naïve &
Abroad**

What is Die Spinne?

About 1969 in Cologne - blond, blue-eyed, and Aryan - I was twice invited to join *Die Spinne*.

Die Spinne is an underground Nazi organization dedicated to the establishment of a Nazi Fourth Reich and the elimination of Jews.

I was told Nasser was a member. I was told King Hussein of Jordan was a member. I was told every important Arab leader was a member. I was told important members of the West German government were members. I was told influential Americans were members.

I was told Otto Skorzeny was head of *Die Spinne*.

About 1965, a German-Argentine friend visited Spain. She stayed in Skorzeny's Madrid apartment.

In the entry to Skorzeny's apartment were photographs of the Third Reich leadership. Every photograph but Hitler's had a black stripe across it. Hitler's photograph had a red stripe across it.

Skorzeny was not in town. I did not meet him.

Not to the point here, but Borman's photograph was not in the group. I believe Borman was Stalin's man in the Führer Bunker. Perhaps

Skorzeny believed that as well. Borman is a story for another book.

When I visited Argentina, the friend introduced me to her new husband, a Latvian Jew. He spoke eloquently of the perils of being a Jew in pre-war Riga. The marriage did not last.

Skorzeny was tried at Nürnberg, but not convicted.

In his autobiography, Skorkeny tells nothing. Skorzeny tells amusing stories about his affair with Eva Peron. Juan Peron did not care. Juan was a pedophile.

In Stuttgart, I met another Colonel tried at Nürnberg and not convicted.

Die Spinne lives quietly underground in Germany, in Belgium, in Austria - especially in alpine Carinthia - in Spain, and throughout Latin America…especially Argentina, Bolivia, and Chile. New generations of Nazis patiently maintain the vigil.

Die Spinne means The Spider in German.

Maybe *Die Spinne* has the Nazi gold.

Most Nazis who reached South America used an underground railroad operated by Caritas, the Catholic relief organization.

Pius XII - the Pope who got the Nazis out - may soon be made a saint.

Pius XII - the Pope who got the Nazis out - may soon be made a saint.

Naïve & Abroad

Is Israel a Nuclear Power?

Yes.

Naïve & Abroad

Why Are Jews So Powerful?

A Muslim's View

There are only 14 million Jews in the world; seven million in the Americas, five million in Asia, two million in Europe and 100,000 in Africa. For every single Jew in the world there are 100 Muslims. Yet, Jews are more than a hundred times more powerful than all the Muslims put together. Ever wondered why?

Jesus of Nazareth was Jewish. Albert Einstein, the most influential scientist of all time and TIME magazine's 'Person of the Century' was a Jew. Sigmund Freud – id, ego, superego – the father of psychoanalysis was a Jew. So were Paul Samuelson and Milton Friedman.

Here are a few other Jews whose intellectual output has enriched whole humanity: Benjamin Rubin gave humanity the vaccinating needle. Jonas Salk developed the first polio vaccine. Albert Sabin developed the improved live polio vaccine. Gertrude Eliion gave us a leukaemia fighting drug. Baruch Blumberg developed the vaccination for Hepatitis B. Paul Ehrlich discovered a treatment for syphilis (a sexually transmitted disease). Elie Metchnikoff won a Nobel Prize in infectious diseases.

Bernard Katz won as Nobel Prize in neuromuscular transmission. Andrew Schally won a Nobel in endocrinology (disorders of the endocrine system; diabetes, hyperthyroidism). Aaron Beck founded Cognitive Therapy (psychotherapy to treat mental disorders, depression and phobias). Gregory Pincus developed the first oral contraceptive pill. George Wald won a Nobel for furthering our understanding of the human eye. Stanley Cohen won a Nobel in embryology (study of embryos and their development). Willem Kolff came up with a kidney dialysis machine.

Over the past 105 years, 14 million Jews have won 15-dozen Nobel Prizes while only three Novel Prizes have been won by 1.4 billion Muslims (other than Peace Prizes.)

Why are Jews so powerful? Stanley Mezor invented the first microprocessing chip. Leo Szilard developed the first nuclear chain reactor. Peter Schultz, optical fiber cable; Charles Adler, traffic lights; Benno Strauss, stainless steel; Isador Iisee, sound movies; Emile Berliner, telephone microphone and Charles Ginsburg, videotape recorder.

Famous financiers in the business world who belong to the Jewish faith include Ralph Lauren (Polo), Levi Strauss (Levi's Jeans), Howard Schultz (Starbucks) Sergey Brin (Google), Michael Dell (Dell Computers), Larry Ellison (Oracle), Donna Karan (DKNY), Irv Robbins (Baskins & Robbins) and Bill Rosenberg (Dunkin Donuts).

Richard Levin, President of Yale University, is a Jew. So are Henry Kissinger (American Secretary of State), Alan Greenspan (fed chairman under Reagan, Bush, Clinton, and bush), Joseph Lieberman, Maxim Litvinov (USSR Foreign Minister, Davis Marshal (Singapore's first chief minister), Issac Isaacs, governor-general of Australia, Benjamin Disraeli (British statesman and author), Yevgeny Primakov (Russian PM), Barry Goldwater, J orge Sampaio (president of Purtugal), John deutsch (CIA director), Herb Gray (Canadian deputy PM) Pierre Mendes (Frency PM), Michael Howard (British home secretary) and Robert Rubin (American secretary of treasury).

In the media, famous Jews include Wolf Blitzer (CNN), Barbara Walters (ABC News), Eugene Meyer (Washington Post), Henry

Grunwald (editor-in-chief Time), Katherine Graham (publisher of The Washington Post), Joseph Lelyyeld (Executive editor, The New York Times, and Max Frankel (New York Times).

At the Olympics, Mark Spitz set a record of sorts by winning seven gold medals. Lenny Krayzelburg is a three-time Olympic gold medalist. Spitz, Krayzelburg and Boris Becker are all Jewish.

Did you know that Harrison Ford, George Burns, Tony Curtis, Charles Bronson, Sandra Bullock, Billy Crystal, Paul Newman, Peter Sellers, Dustin Hoffman,Michael Douglas, Ben Kingsley, Kirk Douglas, Cary Grant, William Shatner, Jerry Lewis and Peter Falk are all Jewish? As a matter of fact, Hollywood itself was founded by a Jew. Among directors and producers, Steven Spielberg, Mel Brooks, Oliver Stone, Aaron Spelling (Beverly Hills 90210), Neil Simon (The Odd Couple, Andrew Vaina (Rambo 1/2/3), Michael Man (Starsky and Hutch), Milos Forman (One flew over the Cukoo's Nest), Douglas Fairbanks (The thief of Baghdad) and Ivan Reitman (Ghostbusters) are all Jewish?

[Dr. Saleem left out Billy Wilder, a Hungarian Jew.]

To be certain, Washington is the capital that matters and in Washington the lobby that matters is The American Israel Public Affairs Committee, or AIPAC. Washington knows that if PM Ehud Olmert were to discover that the earth is flat, AIPAC will makethe 109ᵗʰ Congress pass a resolution congratulating Olmert on his discovery.

William James Sidis, with an IQ of 250-300, is the brightest human who ever existed. Guess which faith he belong to?

So why are Jews so powerful? Answer: Education.

Quoted with kind permission from Dr. Farrukh Saleem, Islamabad, Pakistan

Naïve & Abroad

Appendix I
Middle East Universities in the Top 500

There are seven Middle East universities in the Top 500 worldwide... six in Israel...one in Turkey.

Hebrew University of Jerusalem is No. 65 of the Top 500 Worldwide

Technicon Israel Institute of Technology is ranked between 101 and 151 worldwide

Tel Aviv University is ranked between 101 and 151 worldwide

Weizmann Institute of Science is ranked between 152 and 200 worldwide

Bar Ilan University is ranked between 303 and 401 worldwide

Ben Gurion University is ranked between 303 and 401 worldwide

University of Istanbul is ranked between 402 and 501 worldwide.

These rankings are from the Institute of Higher Education at Shanghai Jiao Tong University. Evidently rankings after the first 100 are in groups.

Turkey is Muslim, but not Arab. Turkey has secular government with separation of Mosque and State.

The Israeli universities are young universities.

Building a Harvard or a Yale, an Oxford or a Cambridge, takes generations.

**Naïve &
Abroad**

Appendix II
Muslim Nobelists

There are 1.4 billion Muslims, two of every ten persons on earth.

Literature

Najib Mahfooz

World Peace

Anwar El-Sadat

Yasser Arafat

Shirin Ebadi

Chemistry

Ahmed Zewail

Physics

Abdus Salam

Norwegian Nobel Committeeman, Kaare Kristiansen, resigned over the Arafat Peace Prize. Mr. Kristiansen said Arafat was a terrorist.

**Naïve &
Abroad**

Appendix III
Jewish Nobelists

There are twelve million Jews, two of every
one thousand people on earth.

Literature

Paul Heyse

Henri Bergson

Shmuel Yosef Agnon

Nelly Sachs

Saul Bellow

Isaac Bashevis Singer

Elias Canetti

Joseph Brodsky

Nadine Gordimer

Imre Kertesz

World Peace

Alfred Fried

Tobias Asser

Rene Cassin

Henry Kissinger

Menachem Begin

Elie Wiesel

Shimon Peres

Yitzhak Rabin

Joseph Rotblat

Chemistry

Adolph von Baeyer

Henri Moissan

Otto Wallach

Richard Willstaetter

Fritz Haber

George Charles de Hevesy

Melvin Calvin

Max Ferdinand Perutz

William Howard Stein

C.B. Anfinsen

Ilya Prigogine

Herbert Charles Brown

Paul Berg

Walter Gilbert

Ronald Hoffmann

Aaron Klug

Herbert A. Hauptmann

Jerome Karle

Dudley R. Herschbach

Robert Huber

Sidney Altman

Rudolph Markus

Walter Kohn

Alan J. Heeger

Irwin Rose

Avram Hershko

Aaron Ciechanover

Economics

Paul Anthony Samuelson

Simon Kuznets

Kenneth Joseph Arrow

Wassily Leontief

Milton Friedman

Herbert A. Simon

Lawrence Robert Klein

Franco Modigliani

Robert M. Solow

Harry Markowitz

Merton Miller

Gary Becker

Rober Fogel

John Harsanyi

Reinhard Selten

Robert Merton

Myron Scholes

George Akerlof

Joseph Stiglitz

Daniel Kahneman

Robert (Israel) Aumann

Medicine

Elie Metchnikoff

Paul Erlich

Robert Barany

Otto Meyerhof

Karl Landsteiner

Otto Warburg

Otto Loewi

Joseph Erlanger

Herbert Spencer Gasser

Ernst Boris Chain

Hermann Joseph Muller

Tadeus Reichstein

Selman Abraham Waksman

Hans krebs

Fritz Albert Lipmann

Joshua Lederberg

Arthur Kornberg

Konrad bloch

Francois Jacob

Andre Lwoff

George Wald

Marshall W. Nirenberg

Salvador Luria

Julius Axelrod

Sir Bernard Katz

Gerald Maurice Edelman

David Baltimore

Howard Martin Temin

Baruch S. Blumberg

Rosalyn Sussman Yalow

Andrew V. Schally

Daniel Nathans

Baruj Benacerraf

Cesar Milstein

Michael Stuart Brown

Joseph L. Goldstein

Stanley Cohen & Rita Levi-Montalcini

Gertrude Elion

Harold Varmus

Erwin Neher

Bert Sakmann

Richard J. Roberts

Phillip Sharp

Alfred Gilman

Martin Rodbell

Edward B. Lewis

Stanley B. Prusiner

Robert F. Furchgott

Eric R. Kandel

Sydney Brenner

Robert Horvitz

Physics

Albert Abraham Michelson

Gabriel Lippmann

Albert Einstein

Niels Bohr

James Franck

Gustav Hertz

Gustav Stern

Isidor Issac Rabi

Wolfgang Pauli

Felix Bloch

Max Born

Igor Tamm

Il'ja Mikhailovich

Igor Yevgenyevich

Emilio Segre

Donald A. Glaser

Robert Hofstadter

Lev Davidovich Landau

Eugene P. Wigner

Richard Phillips Feynman

Julian Schwinger

Hans Albrecht Bethe

Murray Gell-Mann

Dennis Gabor

Leon N. Cooper

Brian David Josephson

Benjamin Mottleson

Burton Richter

Peter L. Kapitza

Stephen Weinberg

Sheldon Glashow

Leon Lederman

Melvin Schwartz

Jack Steinberger

Jerome Friedman

George Charpak

Martin Perl

Frederick Reines

David M. Lee

Douglas D. Osheroff

Claude Cohen-Tannoudji

Zhores I. Alferov

Vitaly Ginsburg

Alexei Abrikosov